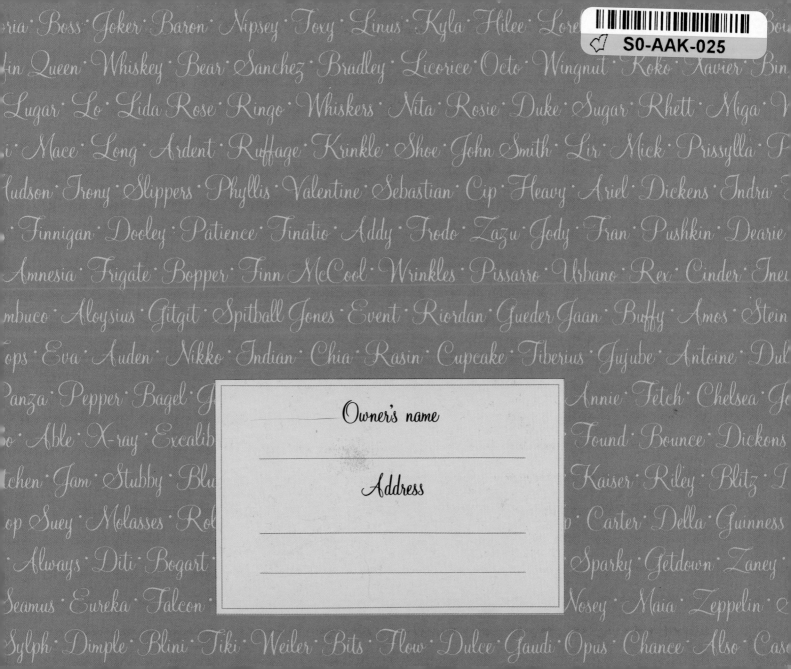

Owner's name

Address

$\mathcal{A}$ puppy is an important part of a household. Just like human babies, puppies will, in time, leave behind their awkwardness and energy, and a little of their sweetness and innocence, and become wise and responsible members of the family.

This book has been created for you to capture, in pictures and words, your dog's brief and magical puppyhood. Later, you can sit with your faithful friend beside you, and smile as you remember.

My Puppy's Record Book

by Alexandra Day & Carl

Farrar, Straus and Giroux
New York

How and When I Got My Puppy

(Classified ad)

Breeder _____

Pound or shelter _____

Pet store _____

Gift from _____

Puppy's age _____

Mother _____

Father _____

Kind of dog _____

Brothers and sisters _____

Why I chose my puppy _____

First Portrait

Photograph

Date _____

Names Considered

Cracker
Buddy Ro...
Mickey
Shannon
Carl(a) Ru...
Chalfont
Jumbo
Smedle...
Max(ine)
Bob
Tromin
Jing...
Cinnamon

Name Chosen

Everyday name _____

Registered name _____

Family Photo

Photograph

Here we are: _____

_____

Date _____

About My New Puppy

Favorite Games and Playthings

Photograph

My Puppy at Play

Date _____

Favorite games _____

_____

_____

_____

Favorite playthings _____

_____

_____

_____

Paw Print

(Use non-toxic poster paint)

Date _____

Lock of My Puppy's Fur

Date _____

Puppy's Schooling

Class we attended _____

Place _____

Dates _____

Teacher _____

What my puppy learned _____

_____

_____

_____

Date of our first walk on a leash _____

Where we went _____

Mealtime

Favorite treats

Bone-hiding places

Stealing and begging anecdotes

Photograph

Date _____

Nap Time

Photograph

Date _____

Bedtime

Photograph

Date _____

Animal Friends

Favorite
People

Un-favorite
People

Record of Growth

Photograph

Four Months Old

Date _____

Record of Growth

Photograph

Six Months Old

Date _____

Record of Growth

Photograph

One Year Old   Date _____

First Holiday

Photograph

TO PUP

Date _____

My Puppy's Tricks

_____

_____

_____

_____

_____

Photograph of
best trick

Date _____

Special Things About My Puppy
Habits, Favorite Activities, Unusual Traits, Likes, Dislikes, Fears

Medical History

My doctor is _____

Address _____

Phone number _____ Date of first visit _____

Immunization History

Date	Type of Inoculation

Weight and Height

	Weight	Height at Shoulders
8 weeks		
10 weeks		
12 weeks		
4 months		
6 months		
1 year		

For Buddy

Thanks to Blake Westman and Darcy vom Rich
for inspiring the "Bath Time" illustration.

rst Dog · Ugo · Radio Flyer · Jambo · Boze · Hawaii · Pronto · Hogan · Abe · Tree · Bows · Os

rince · Von Striker · Patrick · Ubo · Slaker · Von · Hot Shot · Oaxaca · Justice · Motley · Lion

Maggie · Tracker · Nutmeg · Otto · Raisin · Smokey · Aztec · Fudge · Joey · Ebony · Inky · Sun

ebel · Mocha · Murphy · Arff · Jeeves · Pierre · Stoli · Visha · Verve · Jazz · Tara · Eldorado

ooster · Bisquick · Toblerone · Boso · Wingding · Pastrami · Haus · Josephine · Paddy · Gypsy · Er

ndrina · Invictus · Brandy · Gentleman Jim · Floy · Champ · Jumbo · Shannon · Wheezer · Betsy

ckle · Dingo · Back-hack · Fairly · Dragon · Rowdy · Hershey · A.R. · Bede · Gideon · Ride

eroneous · Art · Swartz · Downright · Yago · Chutspah · Siren · Alonzo · Docker · George · Puc

t Deco · Quixote · Morocco · Shadow · Tree · Benny · Winkle · Oddbody · Ella · Adrian · Fai

arley · Akmal · Toast · Grapenuts · Easy · Jazzer · Abby · Dipsey · Sabre · Fire Bird · Eve · San

s · Hector · Alix · Dutch · Masoua · Blintz · Kohl · Silk · Donner · Traveler · Crumpet · Sing

ffles · Foolish · Axis · Extract · Rascal · Dingle · Eunice · Beaner · Griz · Hero · Nero · Eggbert

nicky · Rowley · Nobs · Tanakere · Doofus · Seuss · Cricket · Layla · Eiggy · Zebra · Robby ·

llem · Bingo · Honey · Face Lift · Zimbabwe · Art Nouveau · Conrad · Funny Bone · Ghiradelli

Martha · Feather · Doggy · Smedley · Bonzo · Irish Stew · Cady · Vito · Denney · Best · Pan

underbeat · Candy · Manzo · Volta · Clint · Elbow · Toto · Zeb · Jump · Gael · Dick Tracy · Th